Coffee & Confidence

Lynnecia S. Eley

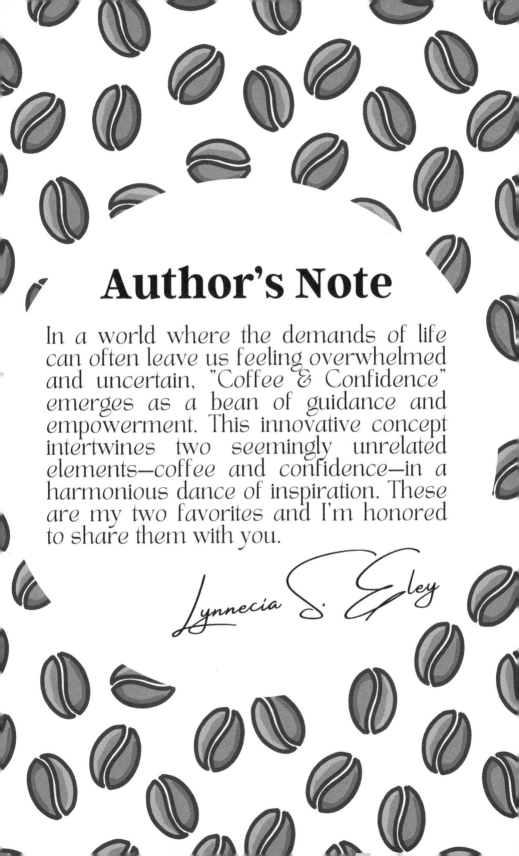

Author's Note

In a world where the demands of life can often leave us feeling overwhelmed and uncertain, "Coffee & Confidence" emerges as a bean of guidance and empowerment. This innovative concept intertwines two seemingly unrelated elements—coffee and confidence—in a harmonious dance of inspiration. These are my two favorites and I'm honored to share them with you.

Lynnecia S. Eley

"COFFEE, BECAUSE ADULTING IS HARD."

Anonymous

No one really knows exactly when or how coffee was discovered, but there are legends about its heritage going back centuries to Ethiopia, East Africa.

An Ethiopian Legend

Coffee grown worldwide can trace its heritage back centuries to the ancient coffee forests on the Ethiopian plateau. There, legend says a goat herder Kaldi first discovered the potential of these beloved beans.

The story goes that Kaldi discovered coffee after he noticed after eating the berries from a certain tree, his goats became so energetic that they did not want to sleep at night. Kaldi reported his findings to the abbot of the local monastery, who made a drink with the berries and found that it kept him alert through the long hours of evening prayer. The abbot shared his discovery with the other monks at the monastery, and knowledge of the energizing berries began to spread.

As word moved east and coffee reached the Arabian peninsula, it began a journey which would bring these beans across the globe.

At its core, this book recognizes the profound connection between the sensory experience of enjoying a coffee beverage and the psychological transformation of cultivating unwavering self-assurance. Just as the careful selection of coffee beans, brewing techniques, and flavor profiles can create a memorable and satisfying drink, the deliberate practice of confidence-boosting tips can craft a life filled with purpose, courage, and determination. The pages ahead take you on a journey where the aroma of coffee mingles with the aroma of self-belief -- inviting you to explore a wide array of quick topics that contribute to a holistic sense of empowerment and affirmation.

The importance of confidence in daily life

Confidence serves as the bedrock on which we build our personal and professional lives.

It is a mental attitude that enters rooms before we physically arrive. It's the driving force that propels us to step outside our comfort zones, pursue our dreams, and engage with people around us. When we lead with confidence, we radiate authenticity and inner strength, allowing us to navigate challenges with grace and resilience.

Whether it's excelling in our careers, building successful businesses, forming meaningful relationships, or embracing new experiences, confidence is the key that unlocks doors to limitless possibilities.

The pages of "Coffee & Confidence" delve into the multifaceted nature of self-assurance, highlighting its pivotal role in enhancing communication, setting and achieving goals, overcoming obstacles, and nurturing a positive self-image. By understanding and nurturing this essential attribute, aka "ATTITUDE", you'll uncover the power to change your interactions, aspirations, and general quality of life.

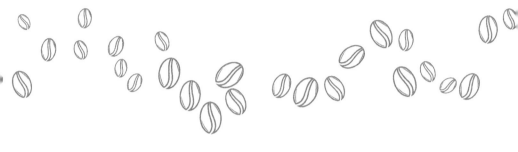

"COFFEEOLOGY: BETTER LATTE THAN NEVER."

Anonymous

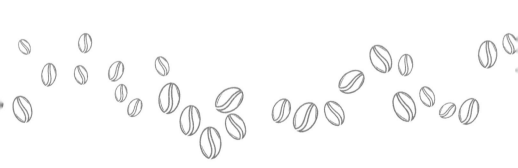

Bold Espresso Shot

Embrace your unique qualities and strengths

Harness the power of self-awareness to identify your inherent strengths and qualities. Reflect on your accomplishments, skills, and the attributes that set you apart. Embrace your individuality without comparison to others. Create a list of your strengths and revisit it regularly, acknowledging your achievements.

By recognizing and celebrating your uniqueness, you'll cultivate a sense of self-assurance and authenticity that shines through in everything you do.

Americano

Set achievable goals and take calculated risks

Dare to dream big while grounding your aspirations in realistic goals. Break your larger objectives into manageable steps, creating a roadmap for success. Be willing to step outside your comfort zone and take calculated risks that align with your goals. Embrace the growth that comes with facing challenges. Each step forward, no matter how small, reinforces your confidence and builds momentum.

Remember, it's not about avoiding failure, but about embracing the process of growth and learning that leads to ultimate success.

Iced Americano

Embrace change and enhance adaptability

Embracing change with an open heart allows you to navigate life's twists and turns with grace. Emphasize the potential for growth that accompanies new situations, and remind yourself that change fosters learning and innovation. Cultivate adaptability by seeking out unfamiliar experiences that challenge your comfort zone. Reflect on past instances where change led to positive outcomes.

This adaptable mindset strengthens your resilience, demonstrating that you're capable of not only weathering change but also harnessing it to propel yourself forward.

Week #3

White-Chocolate Mocha

Challenge and overcome self-doubt

Become an observer of your thoughts, recognizing when self-doubt creeps in. Counter negative self-talk with positive affirmations and evidence of your past accomplishments. Focus on your strengths and potential rather than dwelling on perceived shortcomings. Surround yourself with supportive people who uplift and encourage you. Confront situations that trigger self-doubt, proving to yourself that you are capable of overcoming challenges.

With practice and persistence, you'll rewire your thought patterns and cultivate unwavering self-belief.

Week #4

Improve communication and assertiveness

Enhance your communication skills by actively listening and engaging in meaningful conversations. Practice expressing your thoughts and opinions clearly and respectfully. Embrace assertiveness by valuing your own needs and boundaries while considering the perspectives of others. Remember, effective communication and assertiveness allow you to advocate for yourself and contribute confidently in various settings, leading to stronger relationships and more impactful interactions.

Week #5

"TODAY'S GOOD MOOD IS SPONSORED BY COFFEE."

Anonymous

Chai Latte

Practice mindfulness and prioritize self-care

Engage in daily mindfulness practices, such as meditation or deep breathing, to cultivate self-awareness and reduce anxiety. Prioritize self-care by setting aside time for activities that bring you joy and relaxation. Nourish your body with nutritious food, exercise, and adequate rest. Cultivate a positive self-image by speaking to yourself with kindness and compassion. As you nurture your well-being, you'll not only enhance your confidence but also project a sense of inner strength and vitality that positively influences your interactions and pursuits.

Week #6

Cold Brew

Develop resilience in the face of challenges

View challenges as opportunities for growth rather than setbacks. Embrace a positive mindset and adaptability when confronted with obstacles. Cultivate resilience by acknowledging your emotions, seeking support when needed, and focusing on solutions. Reflect on past experiences where you've overcome adversity to remind yourself of your inner strength.

As you build resilience, you'll approach difficulties with a newfound confidence, knowing that you have the capacity to navigate and thrive in any situation.

Week #7

Enhance networking skills and build relationships

Approach networking as an opportunity to connect and learn from others. Engage in genuine conversations, showing interest in their experiences and insights. Be proactive in seeking out new connections while nurturing existing relationships. Share your own experiences and expertise with authenticity.

Remember, building meaningful relationships is a testament to your interpersonal skills and demonstrates your value within your professional and personal networks.

Master public speaking and effective presentation

Prepare thoroughly for presentations, organizing your content and practicing delivery. Focus on your message rather than fixating on potential mistakes. Utilize techniques like deep breathing to manage nervousness. Engage your audience through eye contact, gestures, and a confident tone of voice. Embrace each speaking opportunity as a chance to showcase your knowledge and connect with your audience.

As you hone your public speaking skills, you'll exude confidence and authority in any speaking engagement.

Macchiato

Practice positive self-talk and affirmations

Harness the power of your inner dialogue by replacing self-doubt with encouraging affirmations. Counter negative thoughts with positive statements that emphasize your strengths and potential. Speak to yourself as you would to a trusted friend, fostering self-compassion. Create a list of affirmations tailored to areas you'd like to boost your confidence in. Regularly recite these affirmations to instill a sense of self-assuredness. By reshaping your self-talk, you'll amplify your confidence and cultivate a nurturing relationship with yourself. Remember, the words you use internally directly influence your external actions and interactions.

Week #10

Drip Coffee

Improve time management and productivity

Organize your tasks and priorities to maximize efficiency and reduce stress. Break larger goals into smaller, manageable tasks and allocate time for each. Minimize distractions and stay focused on the task at hand. Practice self-discipline by setting clear boundaries and avoiding procrastination. Celebrate your accomplishments, no matter how small, to reinforce a sense of achievement. By managing your time effectively, you'll demonstrate your ability to take charge of your responsibilities and approach challenges with unwavering confidence.

Week #11

Cortado

Hone problem-solving skills and make confident decisions

Approach problems as opportunities for growth and development. Break down complex issues into manageable steps and evaluate potential solutions. Use both logical analysis and intuition to guide your decision-making process. Trust your abilities to navigate challenges and arrive at well-informed choices. Reflect on past situations where you successfully resolved problems. By honing your problem-solving skills and embracing confident decision-making, you not only enhance your problem-solving efficacy but also bolster your self-assuredness. This approach sends a powerful message that you're capable of addressing any challenge with clarity and confidence.

Week #12

"COFFEEOLOGY: SO MANY BLENDS, SO LITTLE TIME."

Anonymous

Irish Coffee

Seek feedback and strive for continuous improvement

View feedback as a valuable tool for growth rather than criticism. Seek out constructive feedback from mentors, peers, and experiences. Embrace opportunities to refine your skills and knowledge based on input. Approach mistakes as learning opportunities and acknowledge areas for improvement. By actively seeking feedback and valuing continuous improvement, you demonstrate your commitment to personal and professional growth. This proactive mindset builds your confidence, as you show a willingness to evolve and excel. Remember, the pursuit of improvement is a testament to your dedication and belief in your potential.

Week #13

Mocha Frappuccino

Develop empathy and enhance emotional intelligence

Cultivate empathy by actively listening to others and seeking to understand their perspectives. Put yourself in their shoes to grasp their emotions and experiences. Enhance emotional intelligence by recognizing and managing your own feelings and those of others. Reflect on moments when your empathy positively impacted your relationships. By developing empathy and emotional intelligence, you enrich your interpersonal interactions and self-awareness. This deeper understanding of emotions builds your confidence, as you navigate social situations with sensitivity and communicate authentically.

Strive for balance and manage priorities effectively

Evaluate your commitments and responsibilities to ensure a balanced life. Allocate time for work, relationships, self-care, and leisure. Reflect on how a balanced approach improves your overall well-being. By seeking balance, you demonstrate self-awareness and the ability to prioritize. This organized approach enhances your confidence, as you manage various aspects of your life with intention and poise.

Week #15

Turkish Coffee

Handle criticism gracefully and constructively

View criticism as an opportunity for growth rather than personal attack. Listen attentively to understand the feedback and its intent. Respond with gratitude and curiosity, seeking clarity if needed. Reflect on how past instances of handling criticism positively impacted your growth. By handling criticism constructively, you demonstrate emotional maturity and a growth mindset.

This confident response showcases your ability to receive feedback with humility and use it to refine your skills and character.

Espresso Con Panna
(with cream)

Take initiative and embrace leadership roles

Step into leadership opportunities with enthusiasm. Recognize your unique perspective and the contributions you can make. Initiate projects, share ideas, and lead with integrity. Reflect on times when your leadership made a positive impact. By taking initiative and embracing leadership, you showcase your competence and commitment.

This confident stance inspires others and highlights your ability to lead with conviction.

Week #17

Café au Lait

Resolve conflicts with assertive and effective communication

Conflicts are a natural part of life, but how you handle them can significantly impact your confidence. Practice assertive communication by expressing your thoughts and feelings honestly while respecting others' viewpoints. Avoid aggressive or passive approaches that can undermine your self-assuredness.

Effective conflict resolution entails active listening and empathy, acknowledging the concerns of all parties involved. Seek common ground and strive for mutually beneficial solutions. Reflect on past conflicts where assertive communication led to resolution and strengthened relationships.

Greek Frappé

Embrace failure as a valuable stepping stone to success

Shift your perspective on failure by viewing it as a crucial part of growth. Recognize that setbacks and mistakes are not indicators of inadequacy, but rather opportunities to learn and improve. Embrace a growth mindset, understanding that the path to success is often paved with failures. Reflect on past experiences where failures led to unexpected achievements or insights. Embrace failure as a teacher that guides you toward resilience, adaptability, and innovative thinking. By reframing your relationship with failure, you'll build confidence in your ability to navigate challenges with grace and determination.

Week #19

"SCIENCE MAY NEVER COME UP WITH A BETTER OFFICE COMMUNICATION SYSTEM THAN THE COFFEE BREAK."

Earl Wilson

French Press Coffee

Cultivate patience and persistence in your pursuits

Confidence often flourishes when you exhibit patience and persistence in your endeavors. Cultivate patience by setting realistic expectations and understanding that progress takes time. Embrace setbacks as opportunities to learn and grow, focusing on the long-term goal. Reflect on past achievements that required patience and persistence.

By fostering these qualities, you'll approach your goals with unwavering determination, knowing that persistence and resilience are key ingredients in the recipe for success.

Practice active listening and enhance communication skills

Active listening is a cornerstone of effective communication and a valuable tool for boosting confidence. To truly connect with others, listen attentively, seeking to understand their perspectives without interruption. Validate their feelings and experiences, showing empathy and respect.

Enhance your communication skills by practicing clarity and conciseness in your own speech. Organize your thoughts before speaking and maintain eye contact to convey confidence and attentiveness.

Week #21

Manage stress and anxiety for improved confidence

Stress and anxiety can hinder your confidence, making it essential to develop effective coping strategies. Embrace mindfulness, deep breathing exercises, or meditation to manage stress. Recognize that self-care is not a luxury but a necessity for sustained well-being.

Identify the sources of stress and anxiety in your life, you'll not only enhance your overall well-being but also bolster your self-assuredness. This newfound sense of control over your emotions and responses will enable you to approach challenges with greater confidence and composure.

Week #22

Iced Latte

Recognize the importance of breaks and recharging

In the pursuit of confidence, remember that rest and rejuvenation are vital components. Constant busyness can lead to burnout, which can erode your confidence. Recognize that self-care is not a luxury but a necessity for sustained well-being.

Take short breaks during the day to clear your mind and refocus. Step outside for a breath of fresh air or indulge in a few minutes of mindfulness. You'll approach challenges with a refreshed mind and a resilient spirit, ready to conquer obstacles with confidence and grace.

Boost creativity through play and exploration

Creativity is a powerful ally in cultivating confidence. Embrace playful exploration to unleash your creative potential. Engage in hobbies, art, or activities that allow your imagination to flourish. Reflect on moments when playful creativity sparked innovative solutions or projects.

By nurturing your creative side, you'll not only enhance your confidence but also approach life with a sense of wonder and enthusiasm. Creative expression is a testament to your inner resourcefulness and ability to think outside the box.

Week #24

Caramel Macchiato

Cultivate gratitude and appreciation in daily life

Practice gratitude by reflecting on the positive aspects of your life, no matter how small. Maintain a gratitude journal to document daily moments of appreciation. Express gratitude to others for their contributions to your life. Cultivate mindfulness, allowing you to savor each moment fully. This practice not only enhances your well-being but also reinforces your self-confidence. By focusing on the positive and nurturing an attitude of gratitude, you project an air of contentment and optimism. This confident presence attracts positivity and fuels your belief in your ability to navigate life with gratitude and grace.

Iced Mocha

Discover joy in everyday moments and experiences

Practice mindfulness by savoring the present moment and appreciating small pleasures. Shift your focus from future anxieties to the beauty around you. Keep a gratitude journal to document moments of joy and positivity. Engage in activities that bring you happiness, even in the midst of challenges. As you find delight in life's simple pleasures, you'll cultivate a sense of contentment that contributes to your overall well-being and confidence. This positive perspective will radiate in your interactions, fostering a magnetic and self-assured presence.

Week #26

"YOU'RE
BREW-TIFUL."

Anonymous

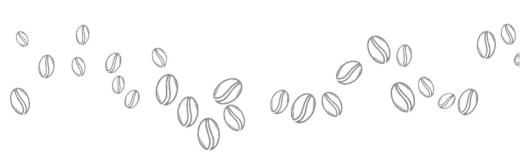

Master body language and nonverbal cues

Nonverbal communication plays a significant role in confidence. Master the art of body language to project self-assuredness. Maintain eye contact, adopt an open posture, and employ gestures that convey confidence and authority.

By aligning your body language with confidence, you'll not only make a positive impression on others but also reinforce your own self-belief. Confidence will radiate from you, and you'll navigate interpersonal interactions with authenticity and poise.

Coconut Latte

Establish and maintain healthy personal boundaries

Recognize the importance of setting boundaries that honor your needs and well-being. Communicate your limits clearly and assertively with others. Prioritize self-care by respecting your boundaries and allocating time for yourself. Reflect on instances where maintaining boundaries led to more fulfilling interactions. By nurturing healthy boundaries, you cultivate a sense of self-respect and empowerment. This confidence radiates in your relationships, showing that you value yourself and your needs.

Week #28

Vietnamese Egg Coffee

Use visualization to manifest your goals and aspirations

Visualization is a powerful tool for boosting confidence and achieving your dreams. Take time each day to vividly imagine yourself succeeding in your goals. See, hear, and feel the details of your achievements as if they're already happening. Visualizing success instills belief in your abilities and aligns your actions with your aspirations.

By consistently practicing this technique, you'll not only bolster your confidence but also increase your motivation to take the necessary steps toward your dreams.

Week #29

Ethiopian Yirgacheffe

Set aside time for reflection and self-assessment

Confidence is closely tied to self-awareness and growth, much like this blend is full of floral and fruit-tones. Dedicate regular moments to reflect on your experiences, choices, and personal development. Self-assessment allows you to recognize your strengths, identify areas for improvement, and set meaningful goals.

By making this a habit, you'll not only deepen your self-understanding but also cultivate a sense of purpose and direction. This newfound clarity will empower you to approach life's challenges with confidence and intention.

Week #30

Vanilla Latte

Cultivate creativity and embrace innovation

Embrace creativity by engaging in activities that inspire and challenge your imagination. Experiment with new ideas and approaches, even if they seem unconventional. Embrace failure as a natural part of the creative process and a stepping stone to innovation. Collaborate with diverse individuals to stimulate new perspectives. Cultivate an environment that encourages creativity by embracing curiosity and open-mindedness. As you infuse creativity and innovation into your endeavors, you'll project a confident, forward-thinking mindset that sets you apart.

Week #31

Strengthen resilience by facing and overcoming adversity

Resilience is a cornerstone of confidence. Embrace adversity as an opportunity to grow and adapt. Reflect on past experiences where resilience led to personal growth and increased confidence. By facing challenges head-on and emerging stronger, you'll not only fortify your resilience but also bolster your self-assuredness.

This resilience becomes a foundation of your confidence, allowing you to navigate life's uncertainties with unwavering resolve.

Nutella Latte

Take affirmative actions to boost your confidence

Confidence often thrives through action. Set clear, achievable goals that align with your aspirations. Take proactive steps to move toward those goals. Reflect on moments when affirmative actions resulted in enhanced self-belief.

By consistently taking purposeful actions, you'll not only increase your confidence but also validate your capabilities. Your accomplishments become proof of your competence and potential.

Week #33

"COFFEEOLOGY: ESPRESSO YOURSELF."

Anonymous

Mexican Café de Olla

Embrace diversity and practice inclusivity

Confidence flourishes in environments that celebrate diversity and inclusion. Recognize the value of different perspectives and backgrounds. Engage in open dialogue and seek to understand the experiences of others.

By embracing diversity and practicing inclusivity, you'll not only cultivate a welcoming atmosphere but also demonstrate your ability to connect with people from various walks of life. This inclusive mindset boosts your confidence, as you navigate the diverse tapestry of humanity with empathy and respect.

Week #34

Indian Masala Coffee

Explore effective time management techniques

Confidence often aligns with effective time management. Discover time management techniques that work best for you, such as the Pomodoro method, to maximize productivity and reduce stress. Reflect on instances when effective time management positively impacted your confidence. By mastering time management, you'll not only enhance your productivity but also project confidence in your ability to manage responsibilities and seize opportunities.

Iced Caramel Macchiato

Practice self-compassion and treat yourself with kindness

Be kind to yourself, especially in moments of struggle. Treat yourself with the same compassion you offer others. Replace self-criticism with self-encouragement. Reflect on times when self-compassion improved your well-being. By practicing self-compassion, you foster a deep sense of self-worth. This self-love enhances your overall confidence and empowers you to navigate challenges with resilience and tenderness.

Week #36

Set goals and prioritize tasks for success

Confidence thrives when you set clear goals and prioritize tasks. Define your objectives and break them into actionable steps. Reflect on moments when goal setting and prioritization led to accomplishments. By consistently setting and achieving goals, you'll not only bolster your confidence but also cultivate a sense of purpose and direction.

This intentional approach to life empowers you to navigate challenges with confidence and achieve your aspirations.

Café con Leche

Cultivate a growth mindset for continuous self-improvement

Adopt a mindset that values effort, learning, and progress. Embrace challenges as exciting opportunities to expand your abilities. Replace self-limiting beliefs with affirmations that reflect your potential for growth. Embrace setbacks as temporary and focus on the lessons they offer. Seek out challenges that push you beyond your comfort zone, knowing that each experience contributes to your development.

As you cultivate a growth mindset, you'll approach life's ups and downs with enthusiasm and self-assurance, confident in your ability to adapt, learn, and evolve.

Week #38

"COFFEEOLOGY:
TAKE LIFE ONE SIP AT
A TIME, AND STAY
GROUNDED."

Anonymous

Almond Milk Latte

Practice mindful eating and adopt healthy habits

Confidence and well-being are intertwined with mindful eating and healthy habits. Pay attention to what you consume, savoring each bite and nurturing your body. Reflect on moments when mindful eating contributed to your overall vitality.

Incorporate balanced nutrition and regular exercise into your routine, as these habits bolster both physical and mental well-being. Recognize that taking care of your body is a powerful way to boost confidence. A healthy body leads to increased self-assurance, as you embody your best self.

Week #39

Piccolo Latte

Craft a compelling elevator pitch to showcase your strengths

An effective elevator pitch is a valuable tool for boosting confidence in professional settings. Craft a concise and engaging introduction that highlights your strengths, skills, and aspirations. Reflect on moments when a compelling elevator pitch positively influenced your interactions.

By mastering this skill, you'll not only make memorable impressions but also project confidence in your abilities. Confidence will flow naturally as you articulate your value succinctly and compellingly.

Cultivate positive habits for a confident and fulfilling life

Positive habits are the foundation of confidence and fulfillment. Identify habits that contribute to your well-being and personal growth. Reflect on times when these habits enhanced your confidence. By nurturing positive habits, you'll not only enrich your life but also cultivate a sense of self-assuredness.

Consistent practices strengthen your belief in your ability to create positive change and navigate life with confidence and purpose.

Week #41

Café Cubano

Overcome procrastination and boost productivity

Break tasks into smaller, manageable steps to minimize feelings of overwhelm. Set specific deadlines for each task to hold yourself accountable. Identify the underlying reasons for procrastination, such as fear of failure or perfectionism. Practice the Pomodoro Technique, alternating focused work periods with short breaks. Celebrate even small accomplishments, reinforcing your sense of achievement. By mastering your time management and overcoming procrastination, you'll foster confidence in your ability to accomplish your goals and take charge of your responsibilities.

Week #42

Cortado con Leche

Craft a personal vision statement to guide your journey

A personal vision statement provides clarity and direction, boosting your confidence as you embark on your life's journey. Take the time to define your values, aspirations, and purpose. Reflect on moments when your personal vision guided you toward meaningful achievements.

By crafting a personal vision statement, you'll not only align your actions with your values but also project confidence in your sense of purpose. Confidence thrives when you have a clear roadmap for your life, enabling you to make decisions and take actions that resonate with your authentic self.

Week #43

Café Bombón

Strengthen inner resilience through self-awareness

Inner resilience is a cornerstone of confidence. Cultivate self-awareness by reflecting on your thoughts, emotions, and reactions. Understand your strengths and areas for growth. Recognize that resilience is built upon self-awareness and the ability to bounce back from adversity.

Nurture these qualities and you'll not only navigate life's challenges with grace but also project confidence in your ability to adapt and overcome. Confidence emanates from within when you know yourself deeply and trust your inner strength.

Week #44

Café Crema

Embrace vulnerability as a source of strength and connection

Understand that vulnerability is a sign of courage, not weakness. Open up about your thoughts, feelings, and experiences with trusted individuals. Share your genuine self, even when it involves admitting imperfections.

Reflect on times when vulnerability fostered deeper connections. By embracing vulnerability and authenticity, you showcase your true self to the world. This genuine approach enhances your self-assurance, as you courageously present your authentic identity.

Week #45

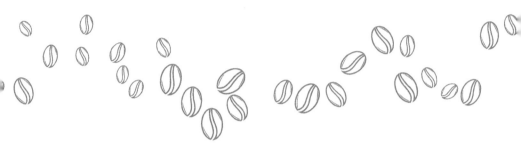

"SOME COFFEE, PLUS SOME THINKING, EQUALS SOME GREAT IDEAS."

Anonymous

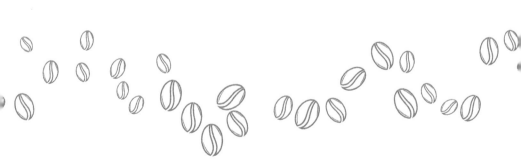

Maple Latte

Harness gratitude to enhance your overall well-being

Gratitude is a cornerstone of confidence and well-being. Cultivate a daily gratitude practice by reflecting on the things you're thankful for. Acknowledge the positive aspects of your life, both big and small. Reflect on how gratitude has elevated your overall well-being.

Confidence grows when you appreciate your strengths and the abundance in your life. A grateful heart becomes a confident heart, ready to face challenges with a positive outlook and resilience.

Week #46

Pumpkin Spice Latte

Pay it forward by sharing confidence and positivity

Confidence is a gift that multiplies when shared. Pay it forward by uplifting and empowering those around you. Encourage others to believe in themselves, and offer support and mentorship when possible. Reflect on moments when your confidence positively impacted someone else's journey.

By sharing confidence and positivity, you'll not only strengthen your own self-assuredness but also contribute to a more confident and empowered community. Confidence thrives when it's a collective force for good, inspiring growth and self-belief in others.

Irish Cream Coffee

Celebrate your achievements and acknowledge your growth

Confidence is nurtured through self-recognition and celebration of your accomplishments. Take time to acknowledge and celebrate your achievements, whether big or small. Reflect on how celebrating your successes has boosted your confidence.

You'll not only build a positive self-image but also deepen your self-belief. Confidence flourishes when you recognize your progress and capabilities. You'll approach future challenges with the assurance that you have the skills and resilience to succeed.

Week #48

"COFFEE - THE FAVORITE DRINK OF THE CIVILIZED WORLD."

Thomas Jefferson

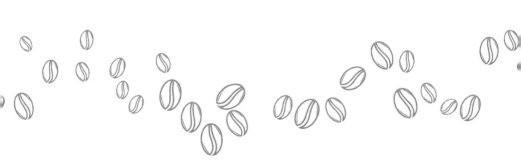

Apple Pie Spice Latte

Develop empowered body language for increased confidence

Recognize the profound impact of body language on how you perceive yourself and how others perceive you. Maintain an open posture, make eye contact, and stand tall to convey confidence and authority. Practice power poses before important situations to boost your self-assuredness. Cultivate a genuine smile that reflects your inner positivity. By aligning your body language with confidence, you'll not only project assurance to others but also reinforce your own sense of self-worth and capability.

Ethiopian Harrar

Expand your horizons by exploring new perspectives

Confidence often flourishes when you embrace diverse viewpoints and explore new horizons. Engage in conversations with individuals from different backgrounds, cultures, and experiences. Reflect on how these interactions have broadened your understanding and enriched your life.

You'll not only enhance your empathy and adaptability but also boost your confidence. Confidence grows when you engage with the world with an open heart and mind, ready to learn from others and share your own unique perspective.

Week #50

Mushroom Coffee

Inspire others through your confident presence and actions

Confidence is contagious and has the power to inspire those around you. Lead by example through your confident presence and actions. Reflect on times when your confidence positively influenced others.

You'll not only uplift those in your sphere but also reinforce your own self-assuredness. Confidence grows when you recognize your capacity to be a source of inspiration and encouragement to others. Your confident leadership becomes a catalyst for positive change, both in your life and in the lives of those you touch.

Week #51

Your Favorite Brew (iced or hot)

Reflect on your journey and continue your path of growth

As you conclude your year-long journey through "Coffee & Confidence," take time for introspection and reflection. Review the lessons learned and the growth achieved. Set new goals and intentions for the future, knowing that confidence is an ever-evolving journey.

Confidence thrives when you embrace the journey of self-discovery and personal development, knowing that it's a lifelong adventure filled with learning, growth, and confidence.

Week #52

Savoring the Blend of Coffee & Confidence

As we reach the end of this journey through "Coffee & Confidence," take a moment to reflect on the path we've embarked upon. Just as each sip of coffee awakens the senses, each confidence tip has stirred the essence of your well-being, invigorating your self-assuredness and setting you on a course of inspiration and empowerment.

Throughout this book, we've explored the intricate interplay between the nuances of coffee and the dimensions of confidence. Each week, a new pairing of coffee and insight has filled both body and spirit, reminding us of the link between the sensory experience of coffee and the growth that confidence offers.

As you close these pages, I invite you to consider how these pairings can be seamlessly stitched into the fabric of your daily life. Just as baristas take the time to select the finest coffee beans and perfect brewing methods, you can apply that same intention to infusing your days with confidence.

Whether you're enjoying a freshly brewed cup or intentionally employing a new found confidence tip, let each moment become an opportunity for self-discovery, growth, and evolution.

Remember, confidence is not a fleeting emotion, but an anchor that accompanies you on your life's journey, an attitude that shows up before you physically do. Embrace your strengths, navigate challenges with grace, and celebrate your achievements, both big and small.

Thank you for embarking on this remarkable odyssey with me. May your cup always be brimming with both your favorite coffee blend and the boundless offering of confidence that resides within you.

Sip,
Savor,
and always walk Confidently!

An Ethiopian Legend
- National Coffee Association of U.S.A., Inc. /
  https://www.ncausa.org/about-coffee/history-of-coffee

Cover Image
- Canva. / Apps, AI: Text to Image

Sources

Printed in the USA
CPSIA information can be obtained
at www.ICGtesting.com
LVHW071130201023
761326LV00087B/130